# HOW TO BE A CREATIVE GENIUS

(in five minutes or less)

HOW TO BE A CREATIVE GENIUS (IN FIVE MINUTES OR LESS)
published by Sherian Publishing

Sherian Publishing
2700 Braselton Highway, Suite 10-390,
Dacula, GA, 30019-3207

To order additional copies, please contact Sherian at:
www.sherianinc.com
1-888-276-6730

Library of Congress Cataloging-in-Publication Data:
Provided by Quality Books, Inc.

Unger, Gary.
    How to be a creative genius : (in five minutes or less) / Gary Unger.
    p. cm.
    LCCN 2007941156
    ISBN 978-0-9795676-2-9
            0-9795676-2-9
            978-0-9795676-3-6
            0-9795676-3-7
    ... [et al.]

    1. Creative ability.  2. Creative ability--Humor. I. Title.
BF408.U54 2008                          153.3'5                          QBI07-600317

# HOW TO BE A CREATIVE GENIUS
(in five minutes or less)

GARY UNGER

S

Atlanta

# HOW TO BE A CREATIVE GENIUS

(in five minutes or less)

# TABLE OF CONTENTS

# ABOUT THE AUTHOR

*"The guy can see around blind corners."* Author, speaker and advertising consultant Gary Unger received this high praise from a client after yet another successful engagement. Gary is a creative powerhouse and gifted humorist driven by his passion to share both gifts with the world. His message is clear: *Be yourself and have fun doing it!* His clever and insightful writing style never fails to inspire laughter and deep thought, helping to unleash the creativity buried in the minds of his readers.

Gary's message has been honed by more than a decade of success in the advertising industry. He is the originator of AutoZone's "Get in the Zone" ad campaign, the longest running ad campaign in the company's history. Gary's creative work has been featured in numerous publications and has also earned him a place in the Levi Strauss T-Shirt Hall of Fame.

A native of Reedsport, Oregon, Gary currently resides in the Atlanta, Georgia area with his wife and three children. To learn more about Gary, visit www.garyunger.com.

# ACKNOWLEDGEMENTS

Thanks to my wife Krista, who keeps me from getting comfortably numb with my failures or successes and encourages me to keep moving forward. This book is also dedicated to my three children who remind me that playing is more lasting than work.

Thanks to Mom and Dad for giving me the book *On Being a Writer* over 20 years ago. Twenty years for it to take affect isn't so bad. Is it?

I'd also like to thank Katina VanCronkhite who selflessly gave time, input, effort and a whole lot of correcting on this manuscript. She has been a great sounding board who can see through my cluttered thoughts and put them into words.

I am also grateful to Phillip Vullo for offering up his input, time, creative ability and excellent photography and to Audra for volunteering her time and talents to an unknown project.

A great many thanks to Monique Moore for getting this in front of Joey Reiman, and for dealing with me. And thank you, Mr. Reiman, for taking the time and lending your name to this little project of mine.

"I used to try and change the world.
Now I change a little for myself"
-Dale Thompson
Bride; I Miss The Rain

# DEDICATION

Dedicated to my wife Krista who sat me down one night and said, "Complete this book even if it doesn't get published."

# FOREWORD

Creativity is intelligence having fun. This cognitive state sets the mind free to travel to imagination's most magical temples, vistas and frontiers. Brains need to come out and play everyday. In this way, our thoughts take wing. The loftier they are, the higher your thinking will soar.

Works of art can inspire us, guide us and restore us. However, to be the artist at work is to have discovered one's purpose and place. Creative people are fortunate for they cannot live without their work. And when one survives only by doing what one loves, one thrives.

Creativity is God's work. You are a creator. That's why we feel so divine when we are lost in our craft. Ironically, we are not lost at all; in fact, this is where we find ourselves. My father left me a note before passing on. It reads: "Creative energy, when not used, turns to depression." Nothing could be truer. Conversely, creative energy, when harnessed, has the voltage to light the world.

Creativity blinds the darkness. Can you ignite creative genius in five minutes or less? Absolutely, if you strike a match. This book is a box of matches.

Joey Reiman
BrightHouse, LLC

Joey Reiman is Thinker, Founder and CEO of BrightHouse, LLC, a global consultancy. He has won more than 500 creative awards in national and international competitions, including the Silver Lion at the Cannes Film Festival. He is a best-selling author of several books, including *Thinking for a Living* and *Success, The Original Handbook*.

www.thinkbrighthouse.com

# GENIUS INTRODUCTION

So you want to be a Creative Genius? Then you've started with the right book. There are many "how to" books on purposeful problem solving already out there. This is not one of them. After all, most creative geniuses rebel at being told how to do something.

## Pass the Salt, Please

When Thomas Edison would interview a potential hire for his lab, he would invite them to have some soup with him. Then he would see if they would put salt on the soup before they even tasted it. If the potential hire did salt before tasting, he wouldn't hire them. Why? Because that person had "unbreakable" habits of not trying things first. Not exactly common HR hiring criteria, then again, look at what came out of Mr. Edison's labs.

This book uses a multi-tiered approach, intermingled with my own "genius" twist combining psychology, philosophy, and humor. Okay, maybe it's sarcasm bordering on the absurd, a character trait that we creative geniuses inherently possess. The purpose is simply to help you understand when you are "salting before tasting" and discover where the creative genius in you needs a bit of tweaking.

## Get It?

With some of the early drafts of this book, I received feedback that "they didn't get it." I assumed the reason they didn't get it was because it was so genius. That, of course, is one of my own lines in this book. Hmm... could I be over salting? So I rethought my approach and now have occasional call out sections called "De Facto" which is philosophy speak for "as a matter of fact."

## About the Check List?

The following check lists of items are humorous, double think, useful, not useful, reverse psychology or sarcasm. Sarcasm makes a great point and often makes you think. What you think is up to you, but you will think. The idea is for you to evaluate yourself, the industry, your creative system or to just laugh at the way we creative types are.

As you read, **_think about the line item that describes any rut or ruts you are in_** (I know, I know, you don't think you're in any ruts) and then find ways to remove that hindrance to your potential creative genius. If you manage people, have your crew take this book home or read it during lunch. Or better yet, schedule a creative meeting to see how every staff member can get more out of themselves than you or they first imagined.

Hopefully you'll get some laughs, gain some personal insights, and buy a few books for other geniuses (with a t-shirt or two). But, most of all, you'll be on the path to being *genius creativus*.

On to the sarcasm.

# GENIUS MENTALITY

❑ Read this book.

❑ Be "for something." Just don't support it.

❑ Demand more money. (Mention you bought this book.)

❑ When attempts at world fame fail, die, and then wait a few years.

❑ Simply act like a genius.

❑ Break not thy habits.

❑ Believe that if less is more, then even less less is
more more.

***De Facto:*** *Water on the Brain.*

When heavy rains pour down repeatedly on a dirt road, they eventually carve out ruts on their way to the lowest point. Your brain operates in a similar way. We humans tend to think reproductively, not productively. That is, when we are faced with a (creative) problem, our responses automatically follow the familiar and previously experienced paths. The good news is that brain ruts can be changed or avoided.

There are three ways to deal with ruts in your mental roads:

1) Don't ever get into one.

2) Recognize them and fight like hell to get out of them.

3) Fall insipidly into one and hope like an idiot it will somehow all be different in the end.

❑ Always wait until the last minute to think about what you are going to do.

❑ Only read the self-proclaimed "hip" magazines.

❑ Think it's ALWAYS about you.

❑ Never eat at a "new" place, unless it is another self-proclaimed "hip" place.

❑ Think rules are for the uncreative.

❑ When the idea doesn't come out right,
blame the budget.

❑ Disregard the mainstream.

❑ Share the workload but never give credit.

❑ If you must read, read only one title on the *New York Times* best seller list per year (the cool one).

❑ Make references to a movie that was only popular to about .03% of the world viewing audience.

❑ Never ever act like an adult. Even if you are 40 and have three kids.

❑ Take the same way *to* work every day.

❑ Take the same way home *from* work everyday.

❑ Assume no one else in the world has a thinking mind.

❑ Only talk to people in your field of work.

❑ Start every sentence with "*I* think."

## *De Facto:* *A Legend in Your Own Mind*

"Pride goeth before a fall," the Good Book says. Good advice for us creative people. We have a tendency to think of ourselves as the only ones with the answer. After all, isn't that why people hire us?

The problem is that even a broken clock is right twice a day and we, as egocentric humans, expand our egos with a type of A Fortiori reasoning.

It goes like this: "If I was right then, how much more right am I now with this?" Humility will do more for your genius than arrogance. Even the big name geniuses throughout history had help and data to back them up.

❑ Never admit that you are wrong – misled maybe, but never wrong.

❑ Only quote philosophers who've been proven to be talking heads.

❑ When negotiating pay or more pay, skip the nuisance insurance part and make sure they have a foosball table in the cafeteria instead.

❑ The more you have to explain your art or idea the better it is.

❑ There is nothing more to learn about art or creativity other than what your art school teacher said.

❑ Always aspire to be someone other than who you are.

❑ Don't balance your checkbook.

❑ Be so demanding that others have to treat you special.

❏ Be vegetarian.

❏ Watch only two TV shows.
   (The others are just time fillers.)

❏ Listen to only one FM radio station.

❏ Never ever listen to a radio talk show unless it is
   a Jerry Springer type show.

❑ Never watch the news.

❑ Be anti-religion.

❑ Believe any weird offshoot ridiculous idea
from the East.

❑ Do drugs.

❑ Be or become single. Only single people can be genius. (Or be at least divorced twice.)

❑ Believe the library is so un-cool.

❑ Be inconsistent.

❑ Have an opinion on everything.

> ### *De Facto:* *It's About the Quantity Stupid*
>
> Pablo Picasso produced over 20,000 pieces. Einstein published nearly 250 papers. Bach wrote music for a full cantata every week.
>
> And you? Not so much?
>
> Genius opens the floodgates and lets ideas flow regardless of feasibility. In fact, many of the works of the great geniuses are not worth printing. But that did not stop them from putting it down on paper and testing them.

❏ Believe you are always right.

❏ Challenge any criticism.

❏ One word: Prima Donna.

***De Facto:*** *Misery Loves Company*

"Misery loves company" is a true and pithy adage, but a more profitable one is "company doesn't love misery." If people seem to be avoiding you, there might be a reason.

Check the altitude of your attitude.

❑ Learn to sigh frequently.

❑ Be eccentric to the point that people leave you alone.

❑ Assume everyone understands your genius.

❑ Never avoid confrontation.

❑ Be tolerant of everyone who has no chance of offending you.

❑ Don't travel.

❑ Equate "controversial" with "genius."

❑ Don't have a sense of humor.

❏ Equate lack of recognition with super genius.

❏ Never take vacation.

❏ Meaninglessness is meaningful.

❏ Never carry cash, credit cards, check book.

❏ Believe contemporary music is the only music for intellectuals.

***De Facto:*** *Video Killed the Radio Star*

Stop, look and listen. You may not have a penchant for certain styles of music, (or art, dance, literature, etc.) but you'll find many commonalities if you explore other tastes.

Part of genius is finding links between things that appear to have no link. Fear of the new is the biggest killer of a better new.

❑ Act like your employer will go under without you.

❑ Have a picture of Einstein on your desk.

❑ Be bland in everything else except your creativity.

❑ It **IS** a mountain, not a molehill.

❑ Poverty is equal to brilliance.

❑ Believe there is nothing wrong with a
   superficial solution.

❑ Don't do anything about your neurosis.

❑ Not neurotic? Fake some type of neurosis.

❏ Don't risk a new trend until it is well established.

❏ Be the loudest voice on a trend that someone else started.

❏ Believe it's their loss if they fire you.

❏ Be condescending.

❑ Only do Pro Bono creative if it helps your book.

❑ Admire some sadistic, murdering "revolutionary" from a third world country.

❑ Have a bad childhood.

❑ Make up a bad childhood.

❏ Use technical terms that no one uses anymore.

❏ Success is not a sign of genius. Ergo...

❏ Whenever you get something – anything – right, it is  because you **ARE** a genius.

# GENIUS DRESS

❏ Be messy in appearance.

❏ Keep your hairstyle even if it is receding.

❏ Wear black as much as possible.

❏ Believe "business attire" should look like a
   Pantone© book of unrelated colors.

### *De Facto:* Dress to Impress

Being in a garage does not make you a car. And wearing a business suit does not automatically grant you the knowledge of an MBA. Neither will dressing "creatively" add any creativity to you.

Psychologists, however, have stated for a long time that dressing up (i.e., business suit or business attire) makes people feel better about themselves. People who feel better about themselves don't listen to negative self-talk as much and are more creatively focused than people who dress as "creative expressions of themselves."

❑ Have a favorite shirt. Limit washings.

❑ Don't groom. It takes too much time away from your genius time.

❑ When posing for your picture, have that thousand yard stare happening.

❑ Wear a "Free Tibet" shirt. Even if you don't know where Tibet is.

❑ Put a "Free Tibet" sticker on your car.

## *De Facto:* *Brain Drain*

Any physical trainer will tell you that the harder you work your muscles the stronger they become. As an added bonus you also get more energy. Your brain is similar. The more you use it, the stronger it becomes. Even trivial musings like what to wear today enhance the brain's thinking capacity.

Variety is the spice of life. It is also the path to genuine genius. Limiting choices and variety so you have more time and brain-power to concentrate on other things is a completely bogus myth.

The less you use your brain, the less your brain becomes of use.

# GENIUS WORK FLOW

❑ Let your graphics program do your designing.

❑ Always carry cocktail napkins around to scribble on, even in meetings. (Napkin ideas are always genius.)

❑ Don't learn to type. Hen peck every time.

❑ Procrastinate.

❏ Spend more than the budget allows.

❏ Get upset whenever there is a change.

❏ Always be obscure about why you'll miss the deadline.

❏ Show up late to work.

❑ Leave work early.

❑ Waste the day. Work through the night.
  (Sleep is for non-genius.)

❑ Believe fast food is made for people like you.

❑ Be obscure when complaining about the creative
  brief being obscure.

❑ If you want something done right, make others feel stupid, then do it yourself.

❑ Keep your door closed.

❑ Clutter your desk with stuff you don't need.

❑ Take notes in a fashion that you won't understand later.

***De Facto:*** *Notebooks Trump Sticky Notes*

Einstein took copious notes and filled up many notebooks on everything he worked on or thought about. "Why try to remember something when you can write it down," he said.

You may think you have a mind like a steel trap, or that sticky notes are considered a memory enhancer. But can you remember the specifics of a problem or subject from one year ago? Two years? Last week? But if you had written it down...

❑ Never bring lunch to work. It allows for longer lunch breaks.

❑ Rationalize an idea to the furthest uncommon connection.

❑ As long as you're not the boss, you're not responsible. Even then...

❑ Always carry stuff you don't use. Everywhere. It'll look like you're an intellectual.

❏ Believe that better equipment equals better ideas.

❏ Self-interest supersedes market data.

❏ Remove any semblance of a filing system.
File drawers should be stuffed, not filed.

❏ If you wear a watch, take out the battery.

❏ Mumble while walking in the hallways.

❏ Have at least one dead plant in your office.

❏ Don't open your mail.

> ### *De Facto:* *Focus Daniel-san*
>
> Despite seeming appearances, geniuses can be very focused. The ability to focus is the main character trait that advances many to genius level. Geniuses have the ability to not get sidetracked by unproductive ideas or distractions and focus on the problems with the most viability and potential.

❑ Think outside the "cubed containment device."

❑ Think so far outside the "cubed containment device" that it takes you back inside the "cubed containment device." It's genius!

❑ Carry more stuff than you can handle into a meeting.

❑ Be award conscious at all times. Forget that "bottom line" thing.

❏ Every room in your home should be your studio.

❏ Stall.

❏ Have assistants do all of your work, but ignore them as a people.

❏ Make hollow promises to others that you are on the verge of a creative genius breakthrough.

❏ Talk about how good the old days were.

# GENIUS HEALTH

❑ Become an alcoholic.

❑ Never wash your coffee cup.

❑ Join a gym, but don't go.

❑ Eat only processed foods.

❑ Believe microwaveable foods show how unconcerned you are with trivial things.

❑ Skip at least two out of three meals per day.

❑ Drink name brand coffee in a branded throwaway paper cup.

❑ Eat quasi-vegetarian in public.

❑ Believe bags under your eyes are your battle scars.

***De Facto:*** *Sleep My Little Pretty*

Remember those war movies where the enemy tortured the good guys by sleep deprivation? Those bad guys knew what we sometimes forget: proper rest is one of the greatest igniters of stamina, creativity and genius. Your brain does lots of creative and restorative processing while you sleep.

Without enough sleep your mind takes "naps" even if you don't. Since the awake part of your mind can't communicate with the napping part, you might as well turn in for the night before total confusion sets in. Sleep is not wasted time. So quit pulling all nighters seeking an epiphany and get some rest.

❑ Party, party, party!

❑ Only drink drinks that have cool names.

❑ Take pills to keep you awake longer.

❑ Become addicted to prescription drugs.

❏ Abuse caffeine when you can't afford the "keep awake" drugs.

❏ Hold in all your feelings.

❏ Embrace, yet struggle with the tortured artist mentality.

❏ Think house cleaning is for lesser people with time.

❑ Believe your car is your home.

❑ Stay seated at your computer working for hours and hours without a break.

❑ Salt before you even taste.

❑ Think Chinese food is life.

❑ Drive, don't walk, to your neighbor's house.

❑ Keep your mountain bike mounted on the wall.

❑ Make sure the computer monitor is only one foot away.

❑ Soft drinks, soft drinks, soft drinks!

❑ ENERGY DRINKS! Coffee is so five minutes ago.

❑ Believe pent up frustration equals fuel.

**De Facto:** *You Are What You Eat*

Some geniuses have had strange nutritional habits (mostly alcoholism or drug addiction), but these habits were the exception and not the rule. And most of their bad habits developed after the big creative break-throughs. Many of the most famous producers in the genius realm like Socrates, Einstein, and Napoleon had relatively healthy nutritional habits.

❏ Ascribe to the theory that coffee and a doughnut make a meal.

❏ Stay indoors whenever possible.

❏ Believe that elevators free up creative time.

❏ Believe that sleep is for the dead.

❏ The faster the life, the better the genius.

❏ Keep stress, keep genius.

❏ Believe that having lots of superficial acquaintances is better than having a few accountable friends.

# GENIUS EXCUSES

❑ They don't get it because it is so genius!

❑ The creative brief didn't mention getting better sales from my ideas.

❑ It was a great idea! I don't know why
   it didn't work.

❑ It's not my fault they don't get me.

❑ I don't need a reason for not having a reason for it.

# GENIUS ADVERTISING

No other industry has the ability to combine art, philosophy, history, sales/marketing, logic and more all in one than advertising. And yet they resort to lazy base concepts and use cookie cutter drivel in an effort to sell us something.

The following is what we allow the advertising industry to feed us when we are unwilling to demand better from these potential geniuses. Keep the following in mind next time you've allowed yourself to be "sold" by mediocre ideas from people who don't think highly of your IQ.

❑ "Offensive to some" is another term for hitting the target market.

*TV Commercials:*

❏ A joke of some nature and scope is always genius.

❏ Put a beach scene in it.

❏ Joe Pytka, Joe Pytka, Joe Pytka!

## *Car Commercials:*

❑ Take a popular song of today or a few years back. Film the car driving on a stretch of curves during spring. Add legal stuff and some voice over. Mix it all together and voila!

❑ Block off a large section of some large city street. Drive the car through it really fast. Have a really cool turning skid filmed. Add voice over and grinding guitar rhythm and you're golden!

❑ Put car in a studio. Show only parts of the car. Never the whole car. That will make people go to a dealership to look at the car. Genius!

### *Drug Commercials:*

❑ Two words: Slice of "make-believe" Life.

❑ Three words: Life Was Hell, then...

❑ Old people always have money.

## _Soft Drink Commercials:_

❑ Sugar water brings people closer.

❑ Men and women can "just be friends."

❑ Add an over-hyped over-exposed pop star.

### *Beer Commercials:*

❑ Think "soft drink commercial" but with beer and the likelihood of sex.

❑ Use underlying deprecating humor.

❑ Think Freudian.

## *Fast Food Commercials:*

❑ Only young, hip, skinny people eat fast food.

❑ Only young, skinny, happy, middle class people work behind the counter.

❑ Think "beer commercial" but with food.

### *High Tech Commercials:*

❏ "My chip can beat up your chip."


❏ Ignore what we said last year and buy this year's or you're a loser.


❏ Show them how "it" will free up their time.

## *Vacation Commercials:*

❑ No one is fat in Vacation Land.

❑ Time doesn't exist in Vacation Land.

## *Services Commercials:*

❑ One word: Motion-graphics.

❑ Think "brochure" but for TV.

### _Computer Graphics in Commercials:_

❑ Computer graphics/animation were meant
to be overdone.

❑ Computer graphics always help weak ideas.

❑ If you can't pull off your idea within the budget,
do it with computer graphics. It's genius.

## *Print Ads:*

❏ Headlines are so passé.

❏ Put a beach in it.

❏ There's no such thing as too little text.

## *Food Print Ad:*

❏ Close up, close up, close up.

❏ Make it a still from the TV commercial. Call it being "cohesive."

❏ Table shot!

*Beer Print Ads:*

❏ Scenic mountain shot.

❏ Two letters: double D's

❏ Sports!

### *Car Print Ads:*

❑ See Car Commercials.

### *Vacation Print Ads:*

❑ See Vacation Commercials.

### *Soft Drink Print Ads:*

❑ See Soft Drink Commercials.

## *Services Print Ads:*

❑ Headlines are never big enough.

❑ Make the logo small. It's about the ad, stupid.

❑ Think "brochure" but on one page.

### *Drug Print Ads:*

❏ See Drug Commercials.

❏ Now is your chance to show Legal how small type can get.

❏ The layout is already copy heavy. Why try to make it nice now?

## *Computer Graphics in Print Ads:*

❏ This is a great time to show how bad it can be done for so little money.

❏ Why photograph reality when you can use the computer?

❏ Genius doesn't do print.

*Internet Ads:*

❏ Make it move.

❏ Make it flash on and off.

❏ Think "billboard" and "TV" mixed into one.

# GENIUS SPICE OF LIFE

So how did you do with the check list? Not so genius? Disappointed? Questioning exactly how to become more creative? That's ok, that's the idea. And there is hope. It just doesn't have a formula. Sorry.

Years of study of genius and creativity have at least revealed one common denominator: variety. Einstein, Mozart, Michelangelo, Disney, Poe, da Vinci, Edison and many like them talked more about variety than any other element in the discovery and thought processes. Walt Disney told a friend concerned about potential investors stealing his ideas, "I can create faster than they can steal." Now that's variety.

Variety is the spice of life. It's also the catalyst for creativity and genius. Variety in volume can help even more. How many different ways can you get to work? Take them ALL. How differently can a TV commercial be done? How many ways can you make tuna fish? Does a brochure have to fold? Can a business card not be flat?

*Don't worry about originality...*

Genius is not in imitating. Genius is focused, deliberate, self aware and continuously uses its brain in a variety of productive ways. Genius asks why, even to its own actions and thoughts.

The great philosopher, theologian and creative genius C.S. Lewis said, "Even in literature and art, no man who worries about originality will ever be original: whereas if you simply try to tell the truth (without caring two pence how often it has been told before) you will, nine times out of ten, become original without ever having noticed it."

Genius ideas don't have to be original. They can be improvements, additions, or insights that no one thought about. Genius looks at all the angles, even the obvious ones.

*The end is here, but the beginning starts now...*

Winston Churchill was a worthy creative genius who spoke the truth, saw the obvious, investigated all the options, broke out of the ruts of his time and became an original. Churchill wrote, "Men stumble over the truth from time to time, but most pick themselves up and hurry off as if nothing happened."

Now you've seen a glimmer of truth. Are you going to walk away as if nothing happened?

Want even more genius?

Contact me at
www.garyunger.com

Photo courtesy phillipvullo.com

Model: Audra Derrick

Order your very own Creative Genius wear!
T-shirts, coffee mugs, and more are available at
www.garyunger.com